W9-BNM-641

SAFETY SMARTS

# SAFE IN THE
# CAR

**PowerKiDS** press
New York

WILLIAM DECKER

Published in 2017 by The Rosen Publishing Group, Inc.
29 East 21st Street, New York, NY 10010

First Edition

Editor: Theresa Morlock
Book Design: Reann Nye

Photo Credits: Cover (background) © iStockphoto.com/welcomia; cover (girl) michaeljung/Shutterstock.com;
p. 5 Alinute Silzeviciute/Shutterstock.com; p. 6 Ronnie Kaufman/Larry Hirshowitz/Blend Images/Getty Images;
p. 9 Balaguta Evgeniya/Shutterstock.com; p. 10 CroMary/Shutterstock.com; pp. 13, 24 (seatbelt) Inti St Clair/
Blend Images/Getty Images; p. 14 Ryan McVay/Photodisc/Getty Images; p. 17 Gladskikh Tatiana/Shutterstock.com;
p. 18 Allen Donikowski/Moment Select/Getty Images; p. 21 Hill Street Studios/Blend Images/Getty Images;
p. 22 Mahatta Multimedia Pvt. Ltd./Corbis/Getty Images; p. 24 (car) Maksim Toome/Shutterstock.com; p. 24 (driver)
Mindscape studio/Shutterstock.com.

Cataloging-in-Publication Data

Names: Decker, William.
Title: Safe in the car / William Decker.
Description: New York : PowerKids Press, 2017. | Series: Safety smarts | Includes index.
Identifiers: ISBN 9781499427882 (pbk.) | ISBN 9781499429886 (library bound) | ISBN 9781499428643 (6 pack)
Subjects: LCSH: Automobiles–Safety appliances–Juvenile literature. | Traffic safety–Juvenile literature.
Classification: LCC TL159.5 D43 2017 | DDC 363.12'5–dc23

Manufactured in the United States of America

CPSIA Compliance Information: Batch #BW17PK: For Further Information contact Rosen Publishing, New York, New York at 1-800-237-9932

# CONTENTS

It is fun to ride in the **car**.

6

We are safe in the car.

We sit in the back seat.

10

Little kids need little seats.

We wear our **seatbelts**.

13

14

Being loud bothers the **driver**.

We keep our hands inside.

17

We do not throw things.

We can take the dog!

21

The car is off. We get out!

# WORDS TO KNOW

**car**

**driver**

**seatbelt**

# INDEX

# WEBSITES

Due to the changing nature of Internet links, PowerKids Press has developed an online list of websites related to the subject of this book. This site is updated regularly. Please use this link to access the list: www.powerkidslinks.com/safe/cars

24